GLORIOUS UNION

Flourishing in marriage and ministry

Adrian and Celia Reynolds

10 Publishing
a division of 10 of those.com

First published in Great Britain in 2016

British Library Cataloguing in Publication Data
A record for this book is available from the British Library

ISBN: 978-1-910587-94-2

Designed by Diane Warnes
Printed in Denmark by Nørhaven

10Publishing, a division of 10ofthose.com
Unit C, Tomlinson Road, Leyland, PR25 2DY, England
Email: info@10ofthose.com
Website: www.10ofthose.com

CONTENTS

SERIES INTRODUCTION

The Hub Conference was launched in 2013 by the Fellowship of Independent Evangelical Churches (FIEC) as an annual conference to help men and women find clear routes into independent church ministry. For those 'just looking' as well as those 'just started', The Hub aims to be one means of support and advice on a possible journey through training and into gospel ministry.

Led by experienced gospel workers from the FIEC, and supported by leaders from colleges and courses, The Hub provides Bible ministry and a wide range of seminars on ministry-related issues.

It is out of this annual conference that this series of books was born. It occurred to the organising committee that these seminar topics could provide a helpful resource for anyone involved in gospel ministry, whether or not they attended The Hub or entered paid Christian ministry. In addition, the hope is that these books might also help pastors and leaders in discipling members of congregations for leadership and ministry.

Someone once described theological books as a *'college of teachers committed to helping you do your best to handle the Word of truth'*. We hope this series will play a small but significant part in that library of wisdom, at whatever stage you find yourself.

Of all the seminars on offer each year at The Hub Conference one of the most popular is always the one on Marriage and Ministry. For a married couple in ministry to not only grow but thrive, their relationship is at the heart of the matter. Which is why we are delighted that Adrian and Celia Reynolds have written this book on this particular subject, coming at is as they do with many years together in marriage and ministry.

Marriage and ministry together can indeed be a 'Glorious Union', as this latest title in our Ministry Journeys series puts it. However, Adrian and Celia are not presenting some idealised utopian dream. They are realistic about the pressures and struggles ministry can bring to a marriage and how to prepare and deal with those difficulties when they arise. It is our prayer and longing that this short book will be of great benefit and use for couples already serving together or looking to serve together in gospel ministry.

Trevor Archer and Dan Green
Series editors

the FELLOWSHIP of INDEPENDENT EVANGELICAL CHURCHES

INTRODUCTION

We always said we would never write a book on marriage. There are far too many already, and we have really very little to say that has not been said at least once. Yet in our defence, this book is a little different. It is not a book about marriage. Neither is it a book about ministry – there are also many of those. Rather, this is a book which we hope is unique: it is a book about the two together. Its focus is not marriage nor ministry, but marriage *and* ministry.

It is worth saying, right from the outset, that our story will not be your story. You can read a little more about our story at the end of this short book, but suffice it to say that your family home will look different from ours: you probably don't have three daughters, and you certainly don't have our three daughters! Your ministry situation will be significantly different from ours. You certainly don't share our particular besetting sins, nor have to work through some of the joys and pains we have had to address.

In other words, this book can only ever be a beginning. We want to get you started to think about some of the issues, but we cannot do the work of application to your specific situation. Only you can do that. For this reason, we have included a workbook at the end, which you could work through together as a start. We also want to encourage you to have another ministry couple that you can pray and talk with: such friendships are invaluable as we seek to minister for the long-term.

Here are some pointers on how to use this book. The first chapter is the longest but we want to encourage you to make your way through all of it as it contains principles to which we will return time and again. It is the least practical of the chapters, but contains the underpinning on which the practical needs to build. We want to ask you to read all the rest of the chapters too. It would be easy, for example, especially if you are struggling, to jump straight to the chapter on pressures or priorities. But to do so and omit the section on privileges would be a mistake. The only way to approach marriage and ministry wholeheartedly and positively is to think about it in its entirety. Too much focus on the privileges without an honest assessment of the pressures will lead to unrealistic expectations. Too much focus on the pressures without remembering the privileges will lead you to self-pity and a begrudging spirit.

There are exercises to do as you go, which means this is less of a book and more of a workbook. If that kind of approach puts you off, then this is not the resource for you. But if you are committed to allowing God to transform you, you will – we trust – find this book a help along the way.

Of course, this is not the last word on marriage and ministry. There are many others who are more experienced than us, and wiser to boot. But we have written this book because of a deep concern about the state of many ministry marriages. It is only by the grace of God, by prayer and by careful planning that our own marriage and the ministries God has entrusted to us have not ended in disaster. So our prayer for you as you read this short book is the same prayer we pray for ourselves: may this be a beginning, and in the glorious grace of Christ Jesus may he take you through to the end.

To the praise of his glorious grace.

Adrian and Celia

OUR HAPPY DAY

The two of us don't always remember things equally clearly. We both remember getting engaged, of course, but one of us remembers the specifics better than the other. One of us can't even remember the precise year. Nevertheless, one thing we *do* both remember is that there was a romantic meal at which we agreed to get married – which we did. The actual day, like many marriage days, was a bit of blur. Again, some details are clear: it was 10 August 1991. Others are more hazy. But we both remember this: we each said, 'I do', and meant it.

But here's the thing: a casual observer might have thought it was all down to us. We agreed to get married. We turned up on the day. We made our promises. At one level, all of this is true. However, in the sovereign goodness of God, we can say something more significant: it is God himself who joined us together. It is this truth which we want to briefly explore in this chapter.

Perhaps more than any other part of this short book, this section will be more of a ministry of reminder. We expect – or at least, hope – that what we want to show you here about marriage will not be new to you.

It should have been part of your marriage prep and, in all probability, is part of the marriage prep you've conducted for countless other couples.

Nor will what we have to show you about ministry be earth-shattering. It's just the same material you've heard many times before. And we need to say right up front that this is not going to be a comprehensive analysis of either marriage or ministry for, as we've already stated, there are plenty of other books that already do that.

However, we do need to establish some baseline principles, so even if this is familiar territory, stick with us. Why? Because just as God joined us together, so he also joined you together: and this truth is at the heart of the ministry and season to which he has called you.

START AT THE VERY BEGINNING

Apparently, according to Maria in *The Sound of Music*, the beginning is 'a very good place to start'. For Christians, that means beginning in Genesis. There are many different ways we could establish some basic principles about marriage; what we're going to do is to pick one Genesis idea and trace it through into the New Testament. It won't take us long, but along the way it will help us work through some fundamentals that every married Christian (and arguably every Christian) needs to know.

Our starting place is Genesis, where God has made everything. He has also made man and woman (Adam and Eve) in his own image and given them a specific role together: 'Be fruitful and increase in number; fill the earth and subdue it. Rule over the fish in the sea and the birds in the sky and over every living creature that moves on the ground' (Gen. 1:28).

This high calling is given to Adam and Eve because they are fundamentally different from the rest of the created order. They are both, together, made 'in the image of God' (1:27). They are not identical; they are 'male and female', both created by a good God. That implies differences which need to be worked out by every couple. (We're not going to say much more about that in this particular book.) Nevertheless, they are both – equally – divine image-bearers and, at some level, it is clear that the divine command in verse 28 is given to them both. A ten-year-old could probably tell you that both need one another – not least to be fruitful and increase in number. They are complementary and yet remain a unit in some way.

That idea is expanded as we read on into chapter 2 and see precisely how God came to make Adam and Eve. Chapter 2 gives us a lot more detail about this specific, special act of creation. Man (Adam) is created first out of the dust of the ground; he comes to life as God himself breathes life into him (v. 7). The question remains, however, how is he to take care of

God's creation, in fact, ruling over it? He's just one man, after all! He needs a helper – someone who will stand with him and work with him, and with whom he can populate the earth so it might be subdued. Given that all of God's creation is repeatedly declared to be 'good' – or even 'very good' – it is striking to read that 'it is *not good* for the man to be alone' (v. 18, my italics). 'Good' here means something like 'fit for purpose'. In all of God's 'fit for purpose' creation something is not right until Eve is created.

No animal can fulfil this purpose. No animal can stand with Adam and it is certainly true that no animal can help him fill the earth. So the writer of Genesis asserts that from amongst all the animals 'no suitable helper was found' (v. 20). Yet the Lord God has a plan! It is to make Eve from Adam and bring her to the man to make the first couple: 'That is why a man leaves his father and mother and is united to his wife, and they become one flesh' (v. 24).

For sure, this is a familiar verse, one that stands right at the heart of marriage from the very beginning. It is, indeed, a very good place to start. We could say an enormous amount about it, but for now – as this is not a marriage book in itself – let's ask a simpler question: how does this foundational truth get used elsewhere in Scripture? That's a useful trail we can pursue. Interestingly, this verse from Genesis appears in the New Testament four times. Two of these occasions are the same story, in essence: the time Jesus is speaking about divorce (or, to be more precise, not divorcing). Then it is used by Paul on two separate occasions. In other words, we have three clear times the verse is used to prove a point by either Jesus or Paul. Let's trace those uses through because, as we shall see, we'll learn three great truths about marriage which will more than set us on our way to getting things right in our minds.

MARRIAGE IS FOR LIFE, NOT JUST FOR CHRISTMAS

First up, Jesus himself quotes Genesis in Matthew 19 (and also in Mark 10). In that particular passage, some of the Pharisees are questioning Jesus about divorce and whether a specific kind of 'no fault' divorce is permissible or not. Jesus answers by quoting two Genesis quotes, both of which we've looked at already.

The first, quoted in Matthew 19:4, is from Genesis 1:27 – that God 'made them male and female'. The second, quoted in Matthew 19:5, is our friend from Genesis 2: 'For this reason a man will leave his father and mother and be united to his wife, and the two will become one flesh.' It is from these two texts (and in particular the second) that Jesus draws his conclusion and answers the interrogators.

His answers are significant. First, the man and woman are one unit: 'So they are no longer two, but one flesh' (Matt. 19:6) – Paul will say something similar in 1 Corinthians 6, as we shall see in just a moment. Secondly, their marriage is a permanent arrangement because it is God who has made them one: 'Therefore what God has joined together, let no one separate.'

These are familiar words to anyone who has ever sat through a wedding service. Jesus is setting Genesis 2:24 in its context. There it is clear that God joins Adam and Eve together. No other creature is suitable for Adam, and therefore God creates Eve specifically to be one with Adam. This first marriage is made in heaven! The same is true, says Jesus, of every subsequent marriage. Jesus, then, has given us two key truths: the two (a man and his wife) are one, and the two are one forever (on this earth, at least).

THE PERFECT WEDDING SNAP

The Apostle Paul also uses the Genesis text, this time in two places. We're going to consider them out of order, because he makes a more general point in Ephesians 5 and a more specific point in 1 Corinthians 6. Let's go to Ephesus first.

In his letter to the Ephesian Christians, Paul has developed a rich doctrine of what it means to be in Christ – something that is both theologically deep and practically abundant. You cannot believe something, he says, without it making a difference in how you live. And so, all through the letter, the riches of what it means to be in Christ are worked out. This practical application begins right at the beginning of the letter, particularly in how it is seen in the church.

It's no surprise, therefore, that these truths are a rich seam of application for specific people in the church: husbands, wives, children, parents, slaves and masters. In a section beginning at 5:21, Paul addresses each (in the full hearing of the other) to tell them what being a Christian looks like. In what is another familiar wedding passage, Paul's instructions begin with wives (vv. 22–24) and husbands (vv. 25–33). Again, a longer marriage book will give you an excellent analysis of these verses and Paul's two specific commands: for wives to submit to their husbands (v. 22) and for husbands to love their wives (v. 25). What we want to see, however, is how Paul uses our Genesis text.

All through this passage he uses the example of Christ and the church to make his points about wives and husbands. Wives are not just to submit to their husbands; they are do so 'as the church submits to Christ' (v. 24). Likewise, husbands are not just to love their wives; they are to do so 'as Christ loved the church and gave himself up for her' (v. 25). Paul is drawing a parallel between the church and Christ, and that parallel is every Christian marriage. Careful Bible readers should not be surprised at this link. After all, throughout the Old Testament the Lord likens his relationship to his people as a husband to a wife, and when his Son – Jesus the Saviour King – comes to earth, he calls himself 'the bridegroom' (Luke 5:34).

Paul makes this implied link explicit in verses 31–32. He quotes the Genesis 2:24 verse and then says, 'This is a profound mystery'. At one point, you can imagine every married couple in the Ephesian church calling out a loud 'Amen' – marriage is indeed a profound mystery! And yet it turns out Paul is not talking about that at all, for he continues, 'but I am talking about Christ and the church.' In other words, our earthly marriages (for that is what they are – there is no marriage in heaven) are pictures of an eternal reality – and that reality is Christ and the church. Our marriages are, in other words, the best marriage snap of all.

It is tempting to read a lot into the language of one flesh – it sounds, after all, like it might refer to sex. We've dealt with this question elsewhere (in our book on sex[1]), but we can see from Paul's language that he must have something deeper in mind. Not every married couple is always able to enjoy sexual intimacy (there are all kinds of reasons why this physical intimacy comes to an end sometimes); and yet the picture still stands. They are still one flesh and their marriage is still, in some measure, a picture of the greater reality.

1. Adrian and Celia Reynolds, *And Then He Knew Her: A biblical view of sex* (Christian Focus Publications, 2015).

DON'T GET HOOKED

Being one flesh is not less than sex, however. Paul makes that clear in the third use of the key Genesis text. It occurs in 1 Corinthians 6. Here, the super-spiritual Corinthians seem to have argued with Paul that their faith allows them to see the body as of being little consequence. As a result, they consider themselves free to do whatever and live however they please. 'I have the right to do anything,' they say (v. 12).

Paul disagrees strongly. The Corinthian Christians are joined to Christ (v. 15) and therefore they are not at liberty to live howsoever they please. So can they, for example, take what is joined to Christ and be united to a prostitute? 'Never!' Paul declares. And why is that the case? 'Do you not know that he who unites himself with a prostitute is one with her in body?' (v. 16). And what is Paul's proof? Yes, you've guessed it: 'For it is said, 'The two will become one flesh.''

In other words, Paul is using a narrower interpretation of one flesh than he did in Ephesians. There, he took one flesh to be indicative of the union the church has with Christ in all its breadth and richness. Here, he narrows in on the immensely private and intimate connection that sexual union brings. Since we are already joined to Christ in the same kind of deep intimacy (not sex itself, but the closeness and intimacy that sex brings), it is unlawful to engage in sexual immorality.

Let's put this all together to build a simple yet profound picture of marriage. We might put it like this: God makes every marriage, joining a husband and wife permanently to be one unit to serve him together and present a picture of Christ and the church. Without going much further, we can see how this is a superb building block for serving in Christian ministry. As we shall see in just a moment, it is not the only one, but nor is it to be despised, for it is glorious.

We've said enough about marriage for now. At the end of this book are suggestions for a few other books you could read which expand significantly on this very brief introduction. Even if this is familiar territory to you, we trust that the old truths have excited you again! God, after all, has brought you together.

SAVED TO SERVE

And what has he brought you together for? Well, assuming you're reading this book because you think it is relevant to you, he has brought you together – at least in part – because Christian ministry is part of who you are as a couple. Precisely what that looks like will be unique to you. It may be that both of you serve in ministry together. Or it may be that Mrs X works in the home, or has paid employment. Perhaps both of you, or one of you, is bi-vocational. There are all kinds of permutations and combinations. But, given that you are in *some* kind of ministry, we need to see some basic Bible truths in order to bring marriage and ministry together in any meaningful way.

There are many places to which we could turn to see the glories of ministry, but perhaps there is no better place than 2 Corinthians 3–4. In this second letter to the Corinthians, Paul is having to defend his own apostleship and ministry. That is because whilst he is away from Corinth, there are some people – whom Paul calls, rather ironically, 'super-apostles' (see 11:5) – who are poisoning the Christians against Paul. This is a serious business because these 'super-apostles' are actually 'false apostles' (11:13). In this context, then, Paul has to launch into an extended defence of his own apostleship. It makes for fascinating reading and encourages us to think deeply about the significance of what Paul himself calls ministry of the new covenant or ministry of the Spirit. Importantly, for Paul, this is a step up from the ministry that was exercised in the Old Testament.

Paul argues that even the great man Moses is eclipsed by what God has given us to do. For sure, Moses had a glorious ministry. How do we know? Well, says the Apostle, people couldn't look at Moses once he had been talking with God (3:7). That's pretty awesome! Who could match that? Actually, he says, everyone who brings the ministry of the Spirit (v. 8). For Moses' ministry was ultimately a ministry that condemned (v. 9). It was still glorious, but it only brought death

(v. 7). Yet 'how much more glorious is the ministry that brings righteousness! For what was glorious has no glory now in comparison with the surpassing glory. And if what was transitory came with glory, how much greater is the glory of that which lasts' (vv. 9–11).

What an extraordinary statement! Moses was *the* great man of God in the Old Testament. He spoke with God as no other did, and such was his ministry that his face physically shone as he ministered to people. Do we think that's impressive? That is nothing, argues Paul, compared to the ministry given to him, and therefore to all who follow in his footsteps. And what is this ministry? It is holding Christ out to people. In 2:14–17, we read that Christ is an aroma that we are holding out to people. Not everyone is going to like it, but that is the task of ministry – offering Christ to men and women. This is the work of the ministry of the new covenant, and it is glorious because it offers life, righteousness and the Spirit.

Just how amazing this ministry is Paul goes on to make clear. In chapter 4 he lists some of the reasons that he might get discouraged. People are not being saved, it seems (vv. 1–6). He feels personally very weak (vv. 7–12). And his own body (as well as those of others) is just fading away with age and use (vv. 13–18). But none of this detracts from the glory that ministry brings. That is why Paul has given his life to 'persuade others' (5:11).

MORE THAN A JOB

What does all this teach us? First, we can say with some confidence that ministry is more than a job. Perhaps we sometimes think of it as a job, as those in ministry might have contracts, salaries and benefits. Perhaps, when we are talking to non-Christian friends, it might seem the easiest way to explain things: 'What's your job?' 'Oh, I'm a minister.' It's one of the drop-down boxes on insurance websites and each year Her Majesty's Revenue and Customs send us a special form headed 'Minister of Religion'.

There are certainly job-like elements about ministry. But it seems from the Apostle Paul's words that it is more than a job.

For one thing, Paul cannot help but do it! 'Christ's love compels us', he writes (5:14). There is a constraint about ministry that every minister should feel. It may, of course, wax and wane. However, on the whole, people should be in ministry because they have to be – not financially, but spiritually.

That sense of burden is expanded further by Paul in his majestic letter. In chapter 11, he explains how his pastoral burden for the Corinthians is inescapable, even from a distance: 'Besides everything else, I face daily the pressure of my concern for all the churches. Who is weak, and I do not feel weak? Who is led into sin, and I do not inwardly burn?' (vv. 28–29).

As we're going to consider later on, it's not that ministry requires longer hours or harder effort than many non-ministry roles. In fact, there will be many in our congregations who work longer hours and consume greater physical resources – there are many, in other words, who need a higher calorie count. Yet there is something about ministry that sets it above these other occupations in the way it drains individuals, especially emotionally. It is more than a job.

That means that even if only one of you is employed in ministry (and the other is perhaps working in the home or in paid employment), you should not think your life will just be the same as everyone else's. That will simply be untrue, unless you are the worst kind of professional pastor. It *is* possible to make it into nothing more than another role in a long list of employment, but those who do don't last very long. They either cannot stay the course themselves or, often more likely, their congregations quickly tire of their detachment. They need a preaching shepherd, not a university lecturer.

BUT YES, STILL GLORIOUS

All of which is to say that ministry is immensely demanding. And yet, remember, it is still glorious. This is Paul's point. He is describing new covenant ministry as greater even than that of Moses. That's how glorious it is. In the next chapter, we'll pause to reflect on that truth, because it is so easy to get caught up in what is hard about ministry that we often neglect to remember what is glorious about it. That's a discipline every ministry couple need to cultivate.

We have now considered marriage and ministry. We've done both briefly, to be honest, but we've seen some fundamental truths. We've seen that every marriage is a one-flesh unit, created by God himself. We've seen that the ministry that brings life is a glorious ministry. Now it's time to put the two together.

MIXING IT UP

There are obviously some very positive things to say. The first is reasonably straightforward. This glorious ministry to which, in all probability, just one of you has been called is something you share in together. You are, after all, a one-flesh unit. Now, we're not arguing for a particular model of marriage and ministry. We're not saying, for example, that a minister's wife must be at home. We simply don't think that is right for everyone. What we are saying, however, is that whatever shape your marriage takes, the work that God has called you to do is one that you both share at some level. That's because you're a union. In fact, any couple who compartmentalise their lives so that they don't share what they are doing with their spouse, at any level, will soon run into difficulties. It's not that you take your husband to work with you, if you are the wife; your work is your work. However, in the theological context of marriage, there is a sense in which it is also his work. He doesn't do the physical job you do, but he shares in it because you and he are one.

That's how married couples should think about ministry. Whatever the wife's role, ministry can never be something that he does alone. Some people might see this as a burden. We've heard wives whose husbands have gone into ministry say something like, 'I didn't sign up for this.' It's sad to hear that, but it reveals a certain mistake – a couple who are considering ministry where one is keen but the other is not should be very, very cautious about taking the step. That is true, in fact, for any decisions made by married couples.

Rather than thinking of this as a burden, ministry couples should think of the joys it brings. As Ecclesiastes 4:12 articulates it, 'Though one may be overpowered, two can defend themselves.' Our own story is that we've sustained each other in the entirety of our marriage – and especially through ministry. Where one has been sometimes foolhardy or precipitous, the other has been wise, and vice versa. Where one has been downcast, the other has been able to lift them up, and vice versa. This is a glorious union.

WHAT DOES THE BIBLE SAY?

Given that marriage and ministry, from our experience at least, is a glorious combination, we might expect the Bible to say something about the union of the two. And it *kind of* does. What does it say? Don't. Did you expect this? That needs a little more explanation. In fact, the Bible never really addresses marriage and ministry. There is, however, a relevant passage for us to look at in 1 Corinthians 7.

There, the Apostle Paul is addressing a particular question that the Corinthians have sent his way: 'It is good for a man not to have sexual relations with a woman' (v. 1). The super-spiritual Corinthians felt that sexual intimacy was a worldly interruption in their higher spiritual pursuit and therefore should be put to one side in sacrifice of the greater good. This is not so, answers Paul. For all kinds of reasons sexual intimacy is key to marriage. Fasting from sex is not on – except in the very rare case where a couple might give themselves to prayer, and even then, only for a short time (v. 5). The Corinthians' question gives rise to an extended section on marriage. Towards the end comes a strongly worded section that seems to suggest that marriage is a bad thing as it complicates life considerably. It is worth repeating in full:

> I would like you to be free from concern. An unmarried man is concerned about the Lord's affairs – how he can please the Lord. But a

> married man is concerned about the affairs of this world – how he can please his wife – and his interests are divided. An unmarried woman or virgin is concerned about the Lord's affairs: her aim is to be devoted to the Lord in both body and spirit. But a married woman is concerned about the affairs of this world – how she can please her husband. I am saying this for your own good, not to restrict you, but that you may live in a right way in undivided devotion to the Lord (vv. 32–35).

What Paul seems to be saying here is that once you get married, your attention is divided. As an unmarried man or woman, you can give yourself wholly to the Lord's affairs. Once you are married, however, your attention is drawn away as you want to please your spouse as well as the Lord.

At one level, this is undeniably true. Adrian's boss, Vaughan Roberts, is an unmarried minister who often says he can achieve a lot more in ministry because he is not married. Paul is stating the reality of marriage and ministry, to which we will return at a later stage.

But it is also important to see what Paul is not saying. It is easy, for example, to read him too negatively at this point. A lot turns on the word 'concerned'. This word can be used in a negative way (to be anxious about something) or it can be used in a positive way (to give one's attention to something). It is clear that Paul is using the word positively here, because he uses it in verses 32 and 34 to describe how an unmarried man or woman is concerned for the Lord's affairs. That is not a nervous anxiety. It is, rather, giving time and energy to the Lord's work.

Paul, in other words, is stating a reasonable and obvious truth: the married man or woman has more things to think about. Their 'interests are divided'. It must be so. It's worth remembering this simple fact. At one level, those who are in ministry and marriage must face up to this truth. There are time demands on married couples that singles don't face in the same way.

It's not, of course, that serving a wife or husband is contradictory to serving the Lord. In fact, the way a husband or wife serves the Lord is precisely by serving and loving their spouse. But that kind of service to the Lord is markedly different from service to the Lord in, say, church. And a sense of reality is good for every ministry couple.

So, it's not so much 'don't do it' – don't combine ministry and marriage – but rather 'if you do, realise that you will necessarily have competing priorities'. That's the reality of marriage, full stop. It's also the reality of marriage and ministry.

BUT YES, STILL GLORIOUS (AGAIN)

Despite the dual demands of marriage and ministry, it's still a glorious combination. Some people have used 1 Corinthians 7 to make an argument for a celibate ministry: that remains the position of the Roman Catholic faith. However, the rest of 1 Corinthians sheds some light on this because both marriage and singleness are described using the Greek word 'charismata', which is the language of gift (v. 7). Marriage is a gift, says Paul, reinforcing what we've seen already from the lips of Jesus himself. It is God who has joined you together.

Furthermore, given that marriage was ordained to make possible the divine command to rule over the earth in Genesis 1, it is no surprise that marriage – whilst not being the only option for those in ministry, nor even the most time efficient – is still a glorious union. Whatever your situation and circumstances, it is something to be delighted in and for which every ministry couple should be deeply, deeply thankful. 'He who finds a wife finds what is good and receives favour from the LORD' (Prov. 18:22).

USE THE WORKBOOK

For this chapter, there's no particular exercise to do, but there are a couple of questions to help you think objectively about your marriage. You'll find them on page 78.

DO NOT FORGET

If you're married, you have a whole load of things to thank God for. Perhaps you don't really feel like it right now, though. Your marriage may be going through a tough patch. There may be more tears than smiles. At such times, it's easy to get so overwhelmed with what's *not* right that you forget everything that is good.

If you're in ministry, you also have a whole load of things to thank God for. Again, perhaps you don't really feel like it. Maybe, like Paul (as we saw in 2 Corinthians 4), you're burdened by the low number of people being saved (if any); maybe it is the inadequacy you yourself feel; maybe it is that you find ministry physically demanding and it is wearing you down. At such times, it's easy to get so overwhelmed with what's *not* right that you forget everything that is good.

Pausing to be thankful is an important Christian discipline. It's a theme, for example, that permeates Paul's prayers in the New Testament. It's there throughout the psalms. Thankfulness is a right response to the work and action of a sovereign and loving God who works all things for our good, which means to conform us into the image of his Son

(Romans 8:28–29). As it is 'in all things', that includes our marriages and our ministry.

So maybe you don't feel like 'counting your blessings', as the old hymn says.[2] Maybe that is something you'd rather save for another day; but you cannot. You must not. Thankfulness is a proper response to the character and nature of God. And this does not mean just vague kinds of thankfulness – a sort of 'thank you God for being loving'. The psalmists, especially, encourage us to be more precise.

We see that clearly in Psalm 103. There David talks to himself and forces himself to remember all that the Lord has done for him: 'Praise the LORD, my soul; all my inmost being, praise his holy name. Praise the LORD, my soul, and forget not all his benefits' (vv. 1–2). David then goes on to list the many benefits for which he must be thankful. Primarily these are forgiven sins, restored health, the glory and honour which befits the anointed king, and steadfast and continued love.

We are not David! We don't live under the same covenant, nor are we anointed kings in quite the same way. Nevertheless, the principle stands. There is a Christian discipline which sets aside the burdens and pressures of the day and takes time to thank God for what we have. 'Devote yourselves to prayer,' writes the Apostle to the Colossians, 'being watchful and thankful' (4:2).

 2. Johnson Oatman, Jr. (1856-1922), *'Count Your Blessings'.*

JOAN OF ARC OLYMPICS?

This is especially true because those in ministry can sometimes compete in a kind of Joan of Arc Olympics. There is a certain type of self-pitying that can become common amongst those in ministry, especially if you're a Brit. Some of our more self-confident American or Australian friends don't seem to suffer from this; maybe it's the weather. However, we've observed that some people in ministry seem to want to outdo one another with just how tough things are.

Sometimes this is a rather macho approach to ministry: 'I haven't had a day off in two months.' Other times it is rather more pitying: 'It's just me which means that I have to do all the admin as well as preaching.' Now, honest evaluation of our lives and ministry is useful and important. We are to think of ourselves 'with sober judgment' (Rom. 12:3). Nevertheless, there is a spirit that delights in competitive pitying amongst many in ministry, and for that reason alone cultivating the discipline of thankfulness is a key practice.

Such thankfulness is important for two reasons. First, it changes our perspectives from being self-centred to being Christ-centred. When we focus on our pressures, we often forget who is in control and what he is like. It's all about me. Or, if we are particularly collegiate, it's all about us. But the discipline of thankfulness is at least one way that ensures we think rightly about life: it's all about him. As the Westminster

Shorter Catechism says, 'Man's chief end is to glorify God, and to enjoy him forever.' It is very definitely not about me. It is the discipline of thankfulness which helps most remedy this misdirection.

Secondly, it is in our human nature to let pressures overwhelm us and loom larger than they ought. There is always a sense of perspective needed. As we are writing, the north of England has been subject to bad floods, with some towns overwhelmed with water. 'We've lost everything' is a common response. Whilst no one would not want to diminish the scale of the disaster, that response is simply not true. Most homes are insured. The Government will step in with emergency help. You might say that such a response from a flooded Bangladeshi villager was more accurate, but certainly it's not true of a flooded northerner, however discouraging the situation may seem.

In other words, pressures make us lose perspective. And it is thankfulness that helps us regain some balance as we reflect on and delight in all the good things that God gives us, and remember that even the things we think of as bad are part of his sovereign will and purpose to make us into his holy people.

CULTIVATING THE JOYS

Where, however, do you start this process of thankfulness? For the purposes of this book, we want to suggest thinking specifically in three areas. Of course, there are many, many things to thank God for (and Psalm 103 is as good a place as any to start). Christians should never dry up! Nevertheless, we're thinking about marriage and ministry in particular, so let's concentrate on those.

Start, first, with your marriage. What is there to thank God for in your union? Even if things are tough, we hope you can make a long list. Be as specific as you like and as private as you like (no one else is going to see this list, after all). God has brought you together. What do you want to praise him for?

Secondly, think about ministry. This may be a harder exercise because perhaps only one of you is really involved in ministry day to day, hour by hour. But, at some level, it's a task you share, and so together you should be able to come up with things to thank God for. There may be specific encouragements or perhaps individuals who come to mind. Or there may be more general circumstances. Either way, you should be able to reel off a long list. What do you want to praise him for?

Then, thirdly, we want you to do something more difficult. What can you praise God for that is related to *both* marriage and ministry? There should be things that come to mind. If you can't think of anything, dare we say you're not thinking hard enough? If you are struggling to come up with ideas, try this: think about how your circumstances are different from other married couples who are not in ministry or other ministers who are not married. Use contrasts, in other words, to prompt your thankfulness.

Perhaps one example might help. We have always tried to have a family meal together in the early evening. When we had busy working lives not in ministry, that was rarely possible. Now, however, it is more of a reality: not every day (ministry is more unpredictable than that), but often. It's one particular thing to thank God for in our marriage and ministry. That blessing might be different for you – but if you are thinking clearly, you should be able to come up with some ideas.

USE THE WORKBOOK

For this chapter, there is an exercise to work through, which you'll find on page 79. We recommend that you do this exercise separately first. Fill in the top two boxes, then think about how marriage and ministry come together by filling in the bottom box. Then share your answers. Some of your responses will be the same. Some will be different. You will see things from different perspectives. However, your answers will help you value one another more, and – perhaps more significantly – nurture a spirit of thankfulness that every Christian ought to have.

You may find it useful to pick just one or two significant items for praise. Perhaps focus on one that is undernourished – you can see it is a privilege, for example, but you haven't really stopped to think about it much or celebrated it or invested in it. Don't just thank God for it, but think through with your spouse what you are going to do to practically cultivate this joy. Possibly it is simply a case of saying, 'Thank you, Lord.' Maybe you need to reshape your lives a little so that this particular privilege takes on more significance?

> **Instead, be filled with the Spirit, speaking to one another with psalms, hymns and songs from the Spirit. Sing and make music from your heart to the Lord, always giving thanks to God the Father for everything, in the name of our Lord Jesus Christ' (Eph. 5:18–20).**

PRESSURES

GETTING PERSONAL

It's time to think about the pressures that being married and in ministry brings. This section, perhaps more than any other, is going to be personal to you. For example, there is a world of difference between a ministry couple where both are in full-time employment and one where only the husband is. It's not that one is more pressured than the others. Rather, it is that the pressures are different.

To be more precise, the pressures that we face are not the ones you face. That is especially true because pressures are sometimes a factor of circumstances and sometimes a factor of character. Often, pressures are a combination of the two. In other words, unless you share our specific besetting sins that we struggle with and unless your life and ministry looks just like ours, your pressures are unlikely to be our pressures.

For sure, there will be some common themes. If we were to outline the struggles we have in very general terms, we would come up with the same sorts of areas. But we are going to encourage you to get specific. You're going to find it hard to biblically address a problem which you describe vaguely as something like 'under time pressure'. In contrast, being more specific will enable you to be more realistic about how, in God's grace, you can see change is possible in this area. So, for example, what kind of time pressure do you face? When? Why? How does it affect others? That's the level at which you need to be thinking.

GETTING HONEST

As well as getting personal, perhaps too now, more than any other time in this book, we need you to be honest. There's no point working at areas that don't really matter. Nor, more seriously, is there much point scratching away at the surface when there are deep issues that remain unresolved and even unmentioned. We're going to suggest a particular way to do that in just a moment, but you need to resolve together as a couple to say what you think and how you feel. There are no resolutions without this kind of truthful dialogue. Too many couples try to fix things based on how they *think* their partner thinks.

GETTING GRACE

This is also the moment to remind you that the Christian faith is one of grace. Addressing problems can be discouraging and the temptation is to descend into a kind of 'I can fix this' attitude. Christians should really have a different mantra: 'God can fix this'. We know you're in ministry, but keep remembering the gospel, as Paul so eloquently describes in Romans 6–7: Christ died for sins and rose again for our justification. He has poured out his Spirit into our hearts and therefore we are no longer slaves to sin but slaves to righteousness, able to say 'no' to ungodliness. God works in us to transform us, but we must not think that this process happens without any effort on our part. God partners with us in our sanctification. Therefore identifying struggles and asking God to help us change, thinking through how that is going to happen, is a very Christian approach. We're not going to say more about that, but there are some suggested resources in the Further reading section if you need them.

It's also worth saying that the gospel of grace is not simply vertical – it doesn't just affect our relationship with God in Christ Jesus. It is also horizontal, and you may well discover that as you work through this section there will be tears and sins to forgive one another. Such forgiveness is at the heart of the gospel (see Matt. 6:14–15). It is also at the heart of every Christian marriage and every Christian ministry. The couple who cannot forgive will always struggle. The minister who constantly bears a grudge will be eaten up with bitterness and fail to serve his people in any meaningful way.

GETTING PERSPECTIVE

It's also worth setting a little perspective before we get going. We wonder how you fared with identifying privileges. When we have run this marriage session for couples in ministry, some really struggle. They are so fixated on what is *not* right, that they struggle to identify anything that *is*. We hope you didn't have that problem. Nevertheless, it is inevitable that it is easier to list problems than it is either to remain thankful or to come up with solutions.

This exercise that we are about to do can therefore be a little overwhelming. So, have a little perspective, please. We're not going to ask you to fix everything at once. Nor are we pretending that perfection comes now. Rather, we're going to encourage you to take some small steps towards resolving some key issues. Keep that in mind as you brainstorm the pressures you face.

GETTING STRUCTURE

To be honest, you can address this area however works best for you. In essence, we want you to identify pressures that you face – particularly those that come from being married and in ministry together. That's where the real pinch point comes. Other books will help if you're struggling in your marriage (see Further reading). Still others will be a help in ministry (though there are less of these). Our concern is primarily about marriage and ministry together. Of course, if there are significant hurdles in one or other, they inevitably bring pressure on the two. But we've found that it's useful if couples focus particularly on the pressures that are unique to your marriage and ministry situation.

There are different kinds of pressures. First, pressures can be different in terms of effect. Some issues create potentially catastrophic outcomes. Some are quite different and are more low level. We want you to identify as many as possible, because even low-level pressures can have a cumulative effect; you sometimes find that a seemingly insignificant issue can take you over the edge because it is the proverbial straw that broke the camel's back.

Secondly, pressures can be different in terms of season. Some are for a relatively short time. Others are long-lasting. Small babies grow up – have you noticed that? So although a tiny baby in the house can be very wearing, those seasons do pass. Other seasons are much longer term – chronic illness, for example.

Thirdly, pressures can be different in terms of how easy they are to resolve. Some are straightforward: if one of you spends too much time on the Internet at the expense of family time, there are relatively simple steps you can take to stop that situation from being out of control. Other besetting sins, like anger, are deep-seated and pulling them out by the roots is both painful and a long-term project.

GETTING GOING

Here is our idea for how to think clearly about pressures. You may find it too complicated or cumbersome – and that's just fine; do whatever works for you. However, if you're struggling to come up with an approach, give the following a try.

In the workbook, we've included a grid with two axes. Up the left hand-side is an axis about how serious the issue is – using our categories above, is it a low-level issue, or a major issue? Distinguishing between the two is useful because at some point you're going to have to pick some to work on. (It's highly unlikely you can pick them all!) If you choose all low-level issues, you'll never get to grips with the major hurdles. If you choose all high-level issues, you'll struggle to get anywhere and then lose heart. So please humour us! Think whether your issues are low or high level.

Then think about whether these issues are straightforward or complex to resolve. Again, this is not to write anything off, but is a way of planning your effort so that, with God's help, you can really make progress. Be realistic about this – if something is going to take some biblical counselling and ten sessions with a mature couple, don't think you can resolve it by reading a blog post.

Then finally we want you to think about whether the issues you've identified are short-term or long-term. What kind of season do they have? You'll have noticed that you've run out of axes on the chart. That's OK. Use two different colours for long-term and short-term. Again, that is a useful way of categorising which will help you make decisions a little way down the line.

If you can, try to think more deeply than how these various struggles present themselves. It is easy to get fixed on symptoms rather than causes. Ask questions like, 'What is the root cause of this issue?' or, 'What sin is giving rise to this conflict?' The more you can get to the root of every issue, the longer lasting the solution is going to be.

When we run this session on conferences or with couples we get them to use Post-it notes. That is a way of being able to move issues around as you discuss them. The end result (in simplified form) looks something like this:

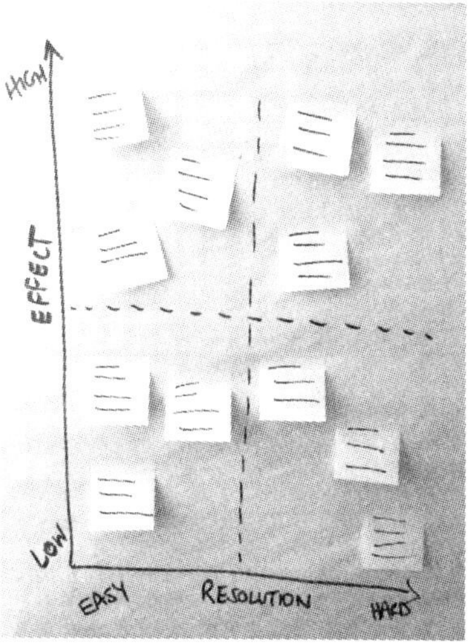

You'll notice that we've split the graph into four quadrants. That's to keep things simple – there's no point doing this exercise and arguing over whether an issue should be ranked as 1 or 2 on a scale of 1–10. This process works much better if you can simply say it is 'low' or 'high'.

Lastly, try completing this exercise separately and then compare answers. Each of you will have some insight that the other lacks, just as – when it comes to resolutions – each of you will have wisdom that the other cannot see.

ONE SLICE AT A TIME

What happens next? Well, you may feel you've done the easy bit, but in fact this first stage is essential. Too many couples in ministry get into difficulty precisely because they cannot be honest about the struggles they face. So, congratulations for getting this far!

The old joke poses the question, 'How do you eat an elephant?' The answer is simple: 'One slice at a time!' And that is the approach you need to take with this chart. Don't feel you have to fix everything straight away. In fact, you're more likely to make progress if you take one or two issues, perhaps four or five at most, and tackle just those. Sometimes, when we've run this session at conferences, couples have chosen just one issue – and that too is fine, especially if it looms large over all the others.

If you are going to choose more than one issue, then try picking them from across the quadrants (and perhaps across the colours if you have used them). For example, in the top left quadrant are what we might call 'easy wins' – they are relatively easy-to-fix issues which will make a significant difference. Why not pick one of these? However, you may find that there are not many pressures listed there. You may find more in the bottom left quadrant – those that are easy to fix but relatively low impact. Choose one anyway! Every step towards godliness is a step in the right direction, and working through some issues which are straightforward builds a sense of confidence in each other and in the Lord's work in you.

However, don't just go for the easy wins. There are some knotty issues on your chart, we would imagine. Don't take on too many of these, but do take on some. There will be real gains here if you're willing to commit, pray and ask God to help you change.

STRUGGLING A BIT?

Perhaps all this seems a bit of a struggle. Here are some ideas to help you.

First, keep applying the gospel to these issues. Think through what the Bible says about them and how the Bible says God works in us by his Spirit to glorify his Son. On this basis, even daunting issues can be addressed.

Secondly, seek help if you need it. If you have a particularly knotty problem and are finding you've reached a kind of stalemate, then meet up with another godly couple. Pray with them and ask them for help. You will almost certainly find that you're not the first couple to struggle in this area.

Thirdly, don't be afraid to be honest. That means you should not be afraid to cry, repent, ask for forgiveness and put yourself on the line. After all, that is what you do when you bring the gospel of Christ to others, and you know, deep down, that is what you must do when you apply the gospel of Christ to yourselves.

USE THE WORKBOOK

The chart to use for this chapter is in the workbook on page 80. You may find you need a bigger piece of paper, in which case simply copy out the axes on to one. As mentioned in the chapter, you may also find it helpful to buy a pad of Post-it notes. Perhaps this kind of exercise seems a little childish or unfamiliar, but trust us that used wisely and in the right spirit, God can use it to help you think clearly and carefully about the struggles you face.

PRIORITIES

DIVIDED LOYALTIES

Every couple knows that what Paul says in 1 Corinthians 7 is right. If you are married, you have to deal with what he calls 'divided loyalties'. In other words, there are tensions because you are not just doing one thing, all of the time. In fact, single or married, no one is. However, when you're married, the simple maths is that you're accountable to more people (plus one!). And when you're in ministry, those responsibility lines are multiplied. Therefore, one of the biggest challenges that many such couples face is of setting and maintaining priorities.

All we can do here is to get you thinking about one or two big issues and to help you avoid making some elementary mistakes. But even a short time thinking about this area will be time well spent. We also encourage you to revisit this topic regularly as priorities in life regularly change as seasons come and go.

FALLING INTO THE TRAP #1

To begin with, there are two huge traps to avoid. These can easily ensnare ministry couples. We want to bring them to your attention because they are not simply based on one or two conversations we've been party to, but are things we hear all the time. This first trap is the danger of setting up a hierarchy of responsibility. It goes something like this (for a husband): I am a Christian first, therefore my primary responsibility is to God; I am husband second, with a responsibility to my wife; I'm a dad third, with responsibilities to my kids; then, and only then, I'm a pastor, with responsibilities to my church.

Now, there is a sense in which there is some truth in this pecking order. But to express it this way is, at best, unhelpful, and at worst, dangerous. Let us explain. For a start, setting our responsibilities to God against our responsibilities in any other area of life is a theological nonsense. Let's think this through by reference to the two greatest commandments.

In Matthew 22, the Pharisees are on the attack. The Sadducees have failed in their bid to unsettle Jesus and now it's the Pharisees' turn: 'Teacher, which is the greatest commandment in the Law?' they ask (v. 36). Jesus' reply is well known: '"Love the Lord your God with all your heart and with all your soul and with all your mind." This is the first and greatest commandment. And the second is like it: "Love your neighbour as yourself."'

In one sense, just like in our list, Jesus is establishing a pecking order. 'The first and greatest commandment' is to love God. Loving neighbour comes second to that. But is there any sense in which loving neighbours is opposed to loving God? Never! The great Christian philosopher Søren Kierkegaard put it something like this: 'Hardly could a more frightful thing be conceived than that there might be a collision between love for God and love for the persons for whom love has been planted by Him in our hearts.'[3] Does loving God come first? Yes, always. But as we love our spouse, our family, our church and others too, we are still loving God. The danger with building a hierarchy of priority is that we miss this obvious point.

In addition, the danger of such a list is that it leads to what we might call, if we were being charitable, unusual behaviour. Take us as an example. We could always work more on our marriage. We could always spend more time together. We could always pray more together. We could always speak to one another more about our days and so on. And if we build a strict hierarchy where we are Christians first, spouses second and so on, then we would never, if we followed those priorities through, get to number three or four on the list. Or, if we did, we would give them so little time or quality attention as to be largely meaningless.

In other words, whilst there may be some truth in the pecking order approach, the very real danger inherent in it is that it leads to skewed decisions about how we spend our time. It is better, in fact, to think of serving God as encompassing a number of areas to which we must be fully committed – marriage and ministry for

3. Kierkegaard puts these words into the mouth of his fictional apologist Judge Wilhelm in *Either/Or*, originally published as *Enter–Eller* in Copenhagen (University Bookshop Reitzel, 1843), p. 249.

starters, but also we might include family and friends and so on. Yes, there will be tensions between these, but setting them over each other in the way many do will lead us to be rather imbalanced people.

In his excellent book on leadership, Craig Hamilton tackles just this point. He encourages us to think about situational priorities rather than static priorities. The trouble with a static list, he says, is that is does not reflect real life. Rather, there is one constant (our priority of Christ first in all things) and everything else settles around this. He helpfully explains this using the metaphor of a lily pond. You may find this illustration slightly forced, but it makes the point well.

> Picture a big circular pond with lily pads floating on the surface. The lily pads that are closer to the centre of the pond are more important than those nearer the edge. The centre of the pond is high priority and the edge of the pond is low priority. Now picture a big rock in the middle of the pond that cannot be moved. That rock is God. He is the centre of your life and will always be your number one priority. Everything you do is in relation to him – what he thinks, what he wants, what he commands.
>
> Everything else in your life is assigned to a lily pad. One lily pad represents your immediate family, another your extended family, another your hobbies. Maybe there's a lily pad for

each different church ministry you lead or are involved in. And so on. What happens is that, as situations and circumstances change, the lily pads float in toward the centre or out toward the edge ... situations almost always govern the order of our priorities. There will never be a situation where God is not the number one priority, so he doesn't move from the centre of the pond. Everything else floats around, depending on the exact and unique circumstances of the moment.'[4]

FALLING INTO THE TRAP #2

Now let's consider trap number two. It relates to one particular issue on the list – that of family. Families are precious things, given by God. All through the Bible they are significant, but the truth is that the family as a significant unit changes as we move from the old covenant to the new covenant. Even those who have the highest view of family would have to agree with that.

It's not that families cease to matter. Rather, it's that the focus shifts. As we move into the new covenant, the lens swings away from single family units and the language of family gets applied in a different way. Indeed, Jesus himself says that he has come to split families apart (Luke 12:51–53) – though presumably only sometimes, not all the time. That is the effect the gospel sometimes has. But there is a new family

4. Craig Hamilton, *Wisdom in Leadership* (Matthias Media, 2015). pp. 95–96.

and it is the local church, the 'family of believers' (a phrase used by both Paul and Peter, see Gal. 6:10, 1 Pet. 2:17 and 1 Pet. 5:9).

Please hear us carefully: it is not that human families cease to be or to have any significance. Plenty is written to address them directly. However, there is a change of balance such that 'brother' and 'sister' are spiritual as much as physical forms of address. As pastor and author John Piper puts it, 'God's family which comes into being by regeneration, is more central and more lasting than the human family that comes into being by procreation.'[5]

It's easy to see how we've ended up at this way of thinking. In general, family life in the UK, where we live, is in breakdown. Nearly all of the vital signs are following a downward trend. Families don't eat together, play together or stay together. Evangelicals who see that God gave us families want to redress the balance. Good. However, we must not do so at the expense of the shift that has taken place where the family of believers is, in God's economy, the chief building block.

How does this relate to marriage and ministry? Simply put, it is possible to idealise and even idolise physical families to the detriment of the spiritual family. Those in ministry are particularly susceptible to this modern evangelical myth – that the physical family counts above all else. If you have children, you probably

5. John Piper, *This Momentary Marriage: A parable of permanence* (IVP, 2009), p. 117.

have more time with them than almost anyone else in the church does with theirs. What a privilege! But you also live to set an example to the flock (1 Tim. 4:12). And therefore you have to maintain a high view of the physical family in the context of the real eternal deal: the family of believers.

WITH ALL YOUR HEART

Once you've avoided our two elephant traps, where next? The reality is you have competing demands on your time and you need to plan for how you will use your limited resources. It's not that these should be set in opposition to each other – as though you can't be a good husband and a good pastor, or a good wife and a good mum or worker. Rather, we need to apply a general principle to all we do.

This is a principle that Paul expresses in slightly different ways in a number of contexts. For example, in Colossians, he uses it in an explicitly work setting: 'Whatever you do, work at it with all your heart, as working for the Lord, not for human masters' (Col. 3:23). In 1 Corinthians, Paul expresses the same wholeheartedness in relation to what our consciences allow us to eat: 'So whether you eat or drink or whatever you do, do it all for the glory of God' (1 Cor. 10:31). The point is essentially the same: the believer's life is one of wholeheartedly giving ourselves to the things that God calls us to, in a way that most glorifies him.

QUALITY NOT QUANTITY

What that means in practice is that we must prioritise our time and our energy. It is simply not sufficient to say, 'I give my best time to my spouse.' When you are in a pastoral meeting with someone, or when you are in the office, or when you are with your kids, it is to those things right then that you are giving yourself wholeheartedly. It would be more precise therefore (though less romantic!) to say, 'I will give some of my best time to my spouse,' and 'I will give some of my best time to my church.'

How do we make those kinds of judgements? At one level, it is cultivating the ability to give our best to different things. We tend to give our best to those things which energise us most. However, it doesn't take long to discover that in both marriage and ministry, and certainly in both together, there are some parts that energise us more than others. So, simply choosing the ones that make us thrive and giving all our energy to those will end up with imbalance again.

Therefore prioritising appropriately is, in part at least, a discipline. That means sometimes voluntarily choosing, in God's power, to be different. We do that with sin; we rightly say to ourselves that, because of our new identity, 'sin shall no longer be [our] master' (Rom. 6:14). We can do the same in a positive way: we can exercise spiritual discipline (which means discipline that comes from the Spirit) to tell ourselves that we will give good quality time to the responsibilities God has given us but that we like least.

USE THE WORKBOOK

The following exercise may help with this prioritisation. Begin the exercise separately. In the workbook (see page 81) set out those various responsibilities God has given you – in any given, normal week – on the left of the page. Obviously life is more complex than this and there are lots of additional pressures that those who are married and in ministry face; but let's keep it simple for now. Try not to be too general, but don't have more than six or seven. Then, in the middle column, jot down the quantity of time you give to these. Perhaps you might write 'start to prepare sermon Monday morning' alongside the responsibility to preach. Then, on the right-hand side, analyse (in very broad terms) whether the quality of this time is usually for you high (i.e. of good quality), medium or low.

Once you have completed this exercise, compare notes and challenge one another. This chart will help you do three things. First, it will help you identify the areas of responsibility that God has given you and to which you need to give yourself wholeheartedly. Secondly, it will show you how much time you're giving to each – something that may need to be challenged. Thirdly, it will help you to see whether you are giving quality time to those areas to which God has called you.

If you're anything like us, this kind of exercise will bring tears, repentance, forgiveness-seeking and prayerful ideas for how to progress.

KINDLING PASSION

A key part of getting marriage and ministry right is to nurture that which is good: 'whatever is true ... whatever is pure, whatever is lovely, whatever is admirable – if anything is excellent or praiseworthy – think about such things', writes Paul to the Philippians (4:8). All Christians should be cultivating the right kinds of attitudes and passions. We've deliberately called this part of the book 'passions' because that is precisely the right word.

Perhaps you don't show much passion. That doesn't mean, of course, that you're not passionate (although it may). It may mean, however, that you have to work harder at convincing your spouse that you're passionate! He or she won't be able to take it for granted, and indeed some problems in marriage arise not because there are particular issues to address, but simply because spouses are poor at communicating exactly how they feel. 'He doesn't love me,' says the wife, missing the fact, for example, that the piece of DIY he's just done is precisely his way of showing his emotion.

We've listed three passions that those who are married and in ministry are called to have. At one level, these are passions that every Christian is called to have, but there is a particular example that we are to set the rest of the flock. So we must not only be thinking and praying about these issues, but others must see that we're making progress in them too.

PASSION KILLERS

Before we get going, it is worth saying that there are some passion killers. That is especially true for those in ministry because ministry itself, if thought about wrongly, can be precisely that – a passion killer. From our own experience, this kind of emotion-sapping is most prevalent when we forget the precise nature of ministry.

Those in ministry are only ever under-shepherds. The flock is not yours; you are simply the caretaker shepherd. It belongs to the Chief Shepherd, the Lord Jesus. Neither is its transformation your responsibility. You are called to minister to this flock and, indeed, to call others into the sheepfold. But if any new sheep join, it is not down to you. And if any of your sheep are made more Christ-like (for which we hope you pray regularly), it only ever happens because God works in them to do his perfect will.

Once you start taking these responsibilities on to yourselves, you are robbing Christ of his glory and his work. And guess what? That's when passion ebbs. That's when your love for God diminishes – why, you wonder, isn't he answering your prayers? That's when your love for each other is strained – why can't you be the man or woman God has called you to be? That's when your love for people is seriously undermined – stupid, stupid sheep! In other words, understanding the key agent behind ministry (the Lord Jesus, working by his Spirit) is essential if you are to avoid killing passions that you are both called to have.

Let's look at the three passions we have identified.

A PASSION FOR GOD

First, and most importantly, every believer is called to love God, '"with all your heart and with all your soul and with all your mind." This is the first and greatest commandment' (Matt. 22:37–38). Interestingly that language – of loving God – is not that common in the Old Testament. Try to find a psalm that expresses it directly, for example. (There are just one or two, like Psalm 18 or Psalm 31.) In fact, the New Testament is similarly reticent about using such language – more often than not the language of love is used to describe how we relate to one another rather than how we relate to God.

There are some notable exceptions, of course, which prove that a passion for God is very much on the agenda. Not only is there Matthew 22 (see above), but we could turn to 1 Corinthians 16:22 or 2 Thessalonians 3:5. Therefore it's not that love for God is unimportant but rather that love for God can be expressed in a myriad of ways. So the Bible is full of expressions of trust or of loving his name or his glory or saying he is worthy. All of these are very common and useful because they all move us beyond mere 21st-century notions of what love is.

In fact, saying, 'I love God' in today's culture could easily be misconstrued to be less significant than it is. Our passion for God is more than a feeling in the tummy, like some kind of love-struck teen. It is deeper, more involved, more consuming. Perhaps that is why, then, that in answering the Pharisees and the Sadducees, Jesus' answer is so rich, invoking the Deuteronomy passage. It could even be translated: 'love with all your heart, *that is* with all your soul and all your mind'.

As you no doubt know, in the Bible the heart is the real you – it's where you think, express faith, treasure memories, derive motives – and so this passion that we are called to have for our Trinitarian God is all-consuming and all-effecting. To say, 'I love God' means, at the end of the day, absolutely everything. It is not to feel gooey about him, but to give him everything and treasure him above all. It is to trust him, believe him, honour him, obey him, listen to him, delight in him and to do so more and more.

And it is precisely this kind of passion that we are called to have. So, a simple question is, do you? Is that your passion? Or has the passion waned away? Perhaps something has happened that has killed it off completely? Perhaps that's the path you're on?

If you are to flourish in marriage and ministry, this must be a passion you cultivate. You cannot afford to let this slip: neither can we. Of course, we all have seasons in the Christian life of ups and downs, but your passion for God is one that cannot be left to flounder like a fish out of water flapping on the dry land.

How can you, therefore, encourage one another in this? Turn to the workbook (see page 82) and jot down some ideas.

A PASSION FOR EACH OTHER

Secondly, we are called to have a passion for one another. We're not thinking here primarily about children or parents or others, but for each other: a husband for his wife, and a wife for her husband. It never ceases to amaze us when we speak to couples in ministry how little they sometimes seem to feel for each other.

Husbands are called to love their wives 'as Christ loved the church' (Eph. 5:25) – a calling which is very high indeed. The corollary of this is often expressed as a wife's submission (Eph. 5:22) and at one level that is right and proper. But wives are also called to love their husbands – that is, after all, what more senior wives are to teach the younger ones in Titus 2. Older wives (having made sure they are not too drunk!) are to 'urge the younger women to love their husbands' (v. 4).

What does this mutual love look like? That, in effect, is the million-dollar question. In one sense, it might seem a more straightforward answer for husbands than it is for wives, because the measure is inserted by Paul into the text. It's to love as Christ loves. But, in fact, the love wives must have for husbands is just the same. How do we know? Well, the love language that all Christians are to have for another is derived from the same place.

That's John's argument running through 1 John: 'We love because he first loved us' (4:19). There is an order to love that connects the love God has for us and the love we are to have for another. But John goes even further. It is not just an order: 'let us love one another, for love comes from God' (4:7). Similarly, 'since God so loved us [by giving his Son], we also ought to love one another' (4:11).

Let us try to explain it another way – what does it mean to love each other? Well, in broad terms, it means to display the same kind of love to one another that God himself has shown for us in Christ. The specifics may differ from couple to couple and from time to time, but in general, the principles always hold true. And that love that God shows to us in characterised in this way:

- It is sacrificial – just as Christ humbled himself, it is putting the interests of the others first.
- It is purposeful – just as Christ gave himself for us, it is doing things for the other person's good; in other words, it is wanting to see them flourish.
- It is proactive and gracious – just as Christ took the initiative with us, so loving our spouse must mean taking the initiative ourselves and not waiting for our partner to do the right thing before we show any love.
- It is quantitatively good – Christ gave himself completely, and so to love a spouse is to give yourself completely to them; that must mean investing in them physically, emotionally, intellectually – at every level, in fact.
- It is qualitatively good – by which we mean to love someone is to not just to give quantity, but quality too. If we're reserving our best for others and not for our spouses, then that hardly seems to be loving in the way God love us, or more precisely, Christ loved the church.

Of course, all of this requires some thinking. How, for example, do we love when we're not at our best – when we're tired or stressed or troubled? How can you, therefore, encourage one another in this? Turn to the workbook (see page 82) and jot down some ideas.

A PASSION FOR PEOPLE

All Christians are called to love other Christians, but it is especially true of those in ministry. A good, healthy ministry marriage should cultivate this love and make it possible. We see that expressed in the shepherd language that the Bible uses to describe Christian leadership. This language (reflected in the word 'pastor') is much neglected today.

For sure, it is correct to call a minister that name (literally, the word means 'a servant'). Paul uses that language from time to time, most notably in 2 Corinthians, but in other places too. However, the overwhelming language of ministry is that of a pastor or shepherd, and that runs like a constant theme throughout the New Testament, indeed throughout the Bible. We mustn't lose that language.

We see the love that shepherds are to have for their people expressed negatively in Ezekiel 34. This is a key passage which will inform the positive point of view which we'll get to in John 10 in just a moment. But the key critique of Israel's shepherds is captured in Ezekiel 34.2: 'woe to you shepherds of Israel who only take care of yourselves! Should not shepherds take care of the flock?' We then get a searing indictment of Israel's shepherds which teaches us a lot about Christian leadership from a negative point of view – it shows us everything shepherding is not. The passage ends with a remarkable promise: 'I myself will search for my sheep and look after them' (v. 11). In other words, I, the Lord, will be the shepherd.

That theme is developed positively in Ezekiel and picked up by Jesus himself in John 10, where he declares, 'I am the good shepherd' (v. 11). There are, of course, aspects of the good shepherd's work that pastors cannot emulate – we cannot atone for the sheep! Nevertheless, the paradigm is right – pastors are under-shepherds serving the Chief Shepherd of his sheep (as Peter puts it in 1 Peter 5:2–4).

And so, we must love the sheep. We must love people. This is ministry, at its most basic. All the other things we treasure and give time to are an expression of this. Preaching, counselling, praying, meeting, directing and so on – these are all elements of what it means to love our people.

Now, of course, this is the requirement for pastors particularly and wives may not feel that they have signed up for this. You are not the pastor; you're married to him – and you may have many cares and worries of your own. There are two answers to that. First, every Christian is called to love other Christians. Therefore, even if the nature and extent of your calling to love is different in some way to that of the pastor, it is still your calling as a believer and you can stand with your husband in this. The second answer is about your marriage itself and takes us back to chapter 1 of this book. You may not be the pastor, but you are married to him. Therefore, as a one-flesh unit, part of your love and service to him is to enable him to fulfil his calling, just as part of his love and service to you is to enable you to fulfil your calling.

So, this issue of loving God's people touches both husband and wife, even though it may manifest itself differently. What do we mean? Well, let's take prayer as an example. The pastor who loves his people prays for his people. Different pastors do that differently but, at the very least, there ought to be a significant commitment to pray for people systematically and regularly. Now, if you're a pastor's wife, you're not called to that same level of giving yourself. But you're still called to love God's people, and therefore it would be very odd if that did not include prayer. So you too should be praying for the church, perhaps using the membership list. But you would be doing it in a different way. Therefore, what we're saying is this: the call to love God's people is a call for both the pastor and his wife, even if it is worked out in the detail in different ways.

Your marriage is an ideal place for this love to flourish. You can help one another to develop this passion. Indeed, you are uniquely placed to spur one another on to love and good deeds. How can you, therefore, encourage one another in this? Turn to the workbook (see page 82) and jot down some ideas.

PROMISES

Now it's over to you! We hope you've noticed that this book has set out to be practical. We don't want simply to fill your heads with ideas; we want you to do something about them. If you've followed the exercises through, there will be lots to reflect on and pray in. There will be things to revisit and reassess. In this very short chapter, we want you to anticipate doing just that. In fact, we want you to make promises to each other.

These are not the kinds of oaths from the Law that Jesus says are no longer necessary (see Matt. 5:33–37) – he is tackling a form of external religiosity which reduces faith down to a series of empty but wordy promises made before God and to God. Instead, says Jesus, Christians are to be trustworthy when it comes to speech.

However, we are still to resolve to do things. Our 'yes' must be 'yes' and our 'no' must be 'no', but there must still be 'yes' and 'no' – especially to one another. Indeed, if you have particularly deep struggles, you will need to hear one another say 'yes' and 'no' in order to be able to make any kind of progress whatsoever.

Exactly what promises you need to make will be your own concern. We cannot tell you, nor even give you guidance. Hopefully, by this stage of the book, you have come up with some concrete things. Don't overreach: it is possible to take too much on and never achieve anything, even trusting in God. Some divine wisdom is called for! But neither should you avoid tackling the deep issues. Some godly ambition is in order!

USE THE WORKBOOK

Look over what you have worked on. Agree on the issues to tackle. Commit them to the Lord in prayer. Ask for godly wisdom and resolve to address them. Seek dependence upon his mighty power. Keep remembering that this power is the power that raised Christ from the dead (Eph. 1:19-20). He has placed enormous power to change at your disposal. In this spirit, and in this spirit alone, make resolutions to one another and together.

There's space to make notes in the workbook – see page 83

A FINAL WORD

Thank you for keeping going through these exercises. When we run these sessions at conferences they seem relatively easy to explain and we can always assist those who struggle with the concepts. In a book, that is a much more difficult task. Nevertheless, we are praying that, with God's help, the ideas and processes we have set out will be helpful as you seek the Lord's transforming power.

Marriage is glorious. To be more precise, *your* marriage is glorious because it portrays the beautiful Bridegroom and his radiant Bride.

Ministry is glorious. To be more precise, *your* ministry is glorious because it brings life as it offers Christ Jesus to people.

The combination is glorious because God has joined you together. He has made you one for this moment and for this task, and that is something to rejoice deeply in.

> **And we all, who with unveiled faces contemplate the Lord's glory, are being transformed into his image with ever-increasing glory, which comes from the Lord, who is the Spirit (2 Cor. 3:18).**

WORKBOOK

In order to make a difference in your marriage and your ministry, you're going to have to invest some time thinking and praying together. Don't imagine you can read a book and – hey presto! – everything is sorted. What we have done here, therefore, is to provide some tools to help you work through the issues raised in each chapter. It's trendy to have discussion questions at the end of chapters of Christian books, but in fact you need something more practical to fuel your thinking and praying. So, for each chapter, here is an exercise you could do to bring things into focus and get you thinking straight.

These exercises are best done in the way we suggest, but if you can think of other ways, that is obviously fine. Where we suggest doing the exercise separately, you could jot down the diagram on a sheet, buy another copy of the book, or feel free to make a photocopy of these pages. (That's not permission to copy the whole book and pass it on to someone!)

PRINCIPLES

For this chapter, simply reflect on this question:

What would other people say about your marriage? Perhaps that might be close friends or church members. If your children are old enough, you could ask them. Perhaps, if you're brave enough, you could actually ask some trusted friends.

Jot down some answers, reflect on them and pray together.

PRIVILEGES

Exercise aim: ***identify the privileges of marriage and ministry, thank God for them and commit to cultivating them.***

Privileges of our marriage

Privileges of our ministry

Privileges of our marriage and ministry together

Use this chart to pray and thank God. Pick one or two key items and think through how you will cultivate these joys.

PRESSURES

Exercise aim: ***identify and evaluate the pressures that you face with a view to selecting some to which you can apply gospel truths.***

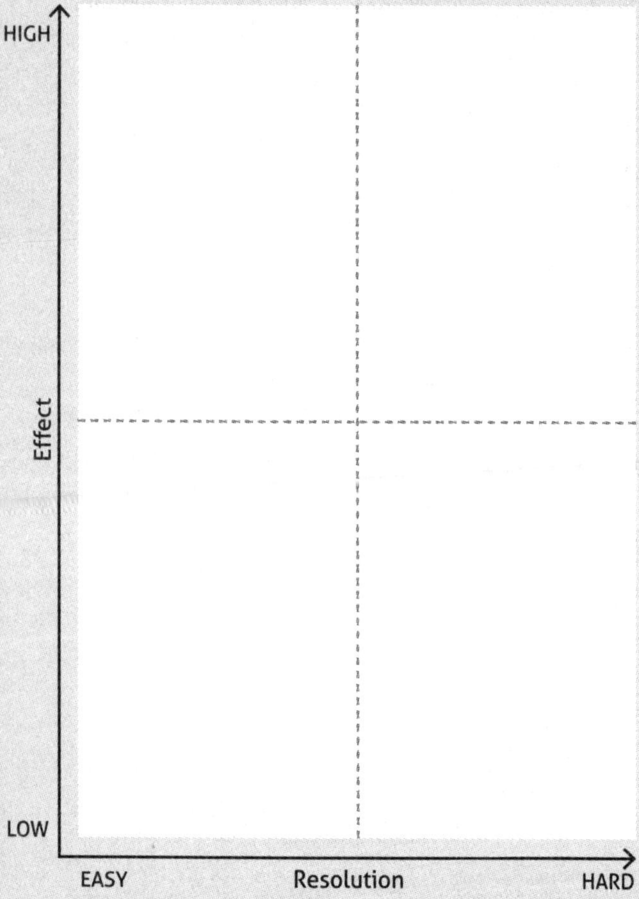

PRIORITIES

Exercise aim: *use this page to evaluate both the quantity and quality of time you give to your God-given responsibilities.*

Responsibility:	Quantity: *what and when?*	Quality:
1.		
2.		
3.		
4.		
5.		
6.		
7.		

PASSIONS

Exercise aim: ***use this page to write down some ideas for how you can encourage one another to develop the right kinds of passions.***

A passion for God

A passion for each other

A passion for people

PROMISES

Exercise aim: *write down what promises you want to commit to, as individuals and as a couple. Set yourself some review dates and return to this list regularly to pray in and act upon what you have decided.*

Resolution:	Review date:

FURTHER READING

In this short section, we want to point you towards a few key books which may be a help in developing these ideas further. There are lots of books on marriage, and almost as many on ministry, so you will find many which we have not included here. However, this list will be useful if you really don't know where to start.

FOR HELP WITH MARRIAGE

This Momentary Marriage: A parable of permanence by John Piper (IVP, 2009).

Strengthening Your Marriage by Wayne Mack (P&R, 2012).

FOR HELP WITH MINISTRY

On Being a Pastor by Derek J. Prime and Alistair Begg (Moody Press, 2013).

The Pastor's Justification by Jared C. Wilson (Crossway, 2013).

FOR HELP WITH CHANGE

You Can Change by Tim Chester (IVP, 2008).

Instruments in the Redeemer's Hands by Paul David Tripp (P&R, 2002).

THANK YOU

We need to say thank you to a few important people. First, we want to express our deep love and thanks to our three daughters, Alice, Bethan and Isabel, who have been with us on our ministry journey and have seen our marriage close up (warts and all) in a way that no one else has. We are also privileged to serve at The Proclamation Trust, a charity that trains preachers and teachers of the Word of God. It has been the vision of the Trust to see investment in ministry marriages as a key element of encouraging and equipping preachers. To this end, it has been a joy to serve on their wives' conferences and – more latterly – on their Marriage and Ministry Stopovers. These were started by David and Heather Jackman and more recently have been continued by Wallace and Lindsay Benn. It is a privilege to build on their key work. Finally, of course, we are thankful to our Sovereign Lord. We know that – on 10 August 1991 – he joined us together, and in his mercy and goodness, no one has separated us (Mark 10:9).

OUR STORY

We were teenage sweethearts! Celia's parents were the local Crusader group leaders where Adrian was converted, and aged fourteen and sixteen (we won't say which way around) we began dating. After university, we married and lived in Hertfordshire, where Celia worked as a primary teacher and Adrian trained as a chartered accountant before working as a training manager and doing a stint at the Serious Fraud Office. Alice and Bethan then arrived, and Adrian moved to work as a senior manager of a pharmaceutical company while Celia worked at home. Next, we moved to Berkshire, and Adrian left business and trained for ministry, beginning to serve at Yateley Baptist Church (in Hampshire) in 2001. Our lovely Isabel was born soon after.

We moved to London in 2009 to work with The Proclamation Trust and take an active part at East London Tabernacle Baptist Church in Mile End. Alice and Bethan grew up and got married. We are now a smaller, but still happy, family with Isabel at home. We're currently in the process of moving again, this time to Market Harborough in Leicestershire, where Adrian is taking up a role as one of the directors of the Fellowship of Independent Evangelical Churches.

Together we have also written *And Then He Knew Her: A biblical view of sex* (Christian Focus, 2005). Adrian has written a number of additional books, including Teaching Numbers (Christian Focus, 2013), *And So to Bed...: A biblical view of sleep* (Christian Focus, 2014) and – in this same series – *To Fly to Serve: Practical help for giving a Bible talk* (10Publishing, 2016).

MORE IN THIS SERIES

ON BEING A SERVANT OF GOD
Warren Wiersbe
978-1-910587-10-2

THE CALL
Trevor Archer & Paul Mallard
978-1-910587-50-8

WHY FREE CHURCH MINISTRY?
Graham Beynon
978-1-910587-49-2

TO FLY TO SERVE
Adrian Reynolds
978-1-910587-60-7

fiec — the FELLOWSHIP of INDEPENDENT EVANGELICAL CHURCHES
10 Publishing — a division of 10 of those.com

To place an order call: **0330 2233 423** email: **sales@10ofthose.com**

or order online: **www.10ofthose.com**

10 Publishing
a division of 10 of those.com

10Publishing is the publishing house of **10ofThose**.
It is committed to producing quality Christian resources that are biblical and accessible.

www.10ofthose.com is our online retail arm selling thousands of quality books at discounted prices.

For information contact: **sales@10ofthose.com**
or check out our website: **www.10ofthose.com**